coastal
AUSTRALIA

Little Hills Press

A wave on the east coast seems to be ignited by shafts of afternoon sunlight.

On the foreshore, foam washes golden sand in this inviting seaside environment.

The Sydney Harbour Bridge is one of Australia's most recognisable structures. Built in the 1930s, it was then described as the 'Iron Lung', for it enabled many families to survive the depression on account of the employment its construction provided. It has long been an icon for the city of Sydney, though since the 1970's it has had to play second fiddle to the Opera House.

Designed by Jan Utzon, The Opera House is a building of vision (especially considering it was selected by an appointed panel of judges on little more than a sketch of its design). Situated on Benelong Point, and surrounded by water on three sides, its sails embrace the harbour. Accentuated here by fading daylight, this landmark is the forefront of a striking cityscape.

Sydney Harbour (Port Jackson) is a deep sea port with gallant heads guarding its entrance. On weekends, its surface carries an interweaving mass of spinnakers and sails. Ocean liners still call into this port, but cargo vessels now generally disgorge their cargo at Port Botany, just south of Port Jackson.

The harbour foreshore, and the islands within the harbour and its outreaches, are national parks or Crown Land, enjoyed by everyone for walking, fishing and swimming.

With so many cities situated on the coast, bridges are very much part of the scenery in Australia. This view of Melbourne is close to the business centre. The Yarra River winds its way along the south of the city as a border between high rise and parkland. The Princess Bridge is a point of congregation for rowers. It traverses the Yarra, linking Flinders Street Station and the city area with the various Art Galleries and parks. Beyond the bridge, looking east, the Melbourne Cricket Ground can be seen, home to Australian football, cricket and the 1956 Olympic Games.

The Storey Bridge in Brisbane, the state capital of Queensland, links Kangaroo Point to Fortitude Valley. Like the Sydney Harbour Bridge, it provided much-needed work during the depression of the early 1930s. During nightime, its lights make it an attractive sight in a city where it is regarded as an icon. Kangaroo Point is now an area of high rise apartments whose Brisbane River views, combined with relatively easy access to the city by road or jet cat, make it a popular dormitory suburb. Fortitude Valley has been undergoing a transformation, with corporate offices replacing warehouses, and swish restaurants, theatres and clubs appearing.

The central business district of Brisbane is situated on a large bend of the Brisbane River. Its flat landform is bounded by water and Spring Hill. New buildings have started to stretch skyward, and the waterfront has now become a site for posh hotels and fine corporate addresses. On the river bank, under the shadow of these new monoliths, restored Edwardian structures, restaurants and pubs, offer a delightful outlook on passing ferries, catamarans and rivercats, and on moored sailing vessels. At the point of the river-bend, both the Queensland University of Technology and the Botanical Gardens give breathing space to a vibrant and developing inner-city centre.

Hobart. Victoria Dock on Hobart Harbour is just to the left of Constitution Dock, which is the finishing destination for boats in the annual Sydney to Hobart Yacht Race. Hobart is the capital of Tasmania and Australia's second-oldest settlement, with a present population of some 200,000 people. One of Australia's finest seafood restaurants, Mure's Upper Deck Restaurant, can be seen here amid fishing vessels. In many ways, this part of Australia is a tranquil retreat, far-removed from the rat-race of major mainland cities.

St Kilda Pier, Melbourne. Situated on Port Phillip Bay. Looking back towards the city skyline of Victoria's capital, Melbourne, the sailing boats of members of the Royal Melbourne Yacht Squadron can be seen moored in this spectacular setting.

For about one week every March, this typically relaxed area is deafened by the sound of high performance engines racing on the Formula One Grand Prix circuit built in nearby Albert Park.

Kodak Beach, South Bank, Brisbane. Originally cleared for the famous international Expo, South Bank is now a combination of parklands and gardens. The Queensland Conservatorium of Music, the Performing Arts complex, the Art Gallery, the Exhibition and Convention Centre, and the Museum, together with many restaurants and theatres, are located nearby.

Beach near Ulladulla, New South Wales south coast. This tranquil scene is repeated throughout the coast of Australia. Australia's coastline is blessed almost universally with white soft sandy beaches.

When travelling along the coast, stop and enjoy your own piece of heaven miles from anywhere and anyone.

Though Coogee Beach on Sydney's south side tends to have a smaller swell because of the bombora 500 metres from the shore, the promenade and park

together with the restaurants and hotels make it a popular place to go for an evening stroll or a surf.

disarming, but sunscreen lotion, glasses and a hat should always be worn beneath the fierce Australian sun. If you are not among those avid amphibians riding surfboards or 'boogy-boards', then try flippers as a great asset for catching Sydney's waves.

Manly Beach on Sydney's north is frequented throughout the year by local Sydneysiders, people from the country, and interstate and overseas visitors.

Fringed by a headland to the South and North Steyne beach at the other end, it is one of 19 beaches in the metropolitan area north of Sydney Harbour.

A view of Shute Harbour in Queensland's far north. Many cruises leave here on voyages to the Whitsundays, a group of islands near the Great Barrier Reef. The picturesque area offers its own vivid attractions, so some travellers prefer to stay on the mainland and go on day trips out to the reef.

Young explorers
scavenge among rock
pools on the sunny
Queensland coast.
The moist, salty sand
of this secluded inlet,
combined with a sultry
climate, allows
mangrove trees to
flourish.

Boats moored in the Great Barrier Reef region. The reef extends 2030km from Breaksea Spit on the Queensland coast of Australia, south of the Tropic of Capricorn to the coastal waters of Papua New Guinea. Thousands of atolls, islands and shoals, reefs and coral formations combine to form an incredible natural wonder; a calm underwater world of stunning colour and sea life.

Coconut Grove, Airlie Beach, Great Barrier Reef, Queensland. A yacht beached on the shoreline of Coconut Grove is surrounded by *everything that inspires visions of paradise: palm trees, forested mountain slopes and water as blue and calm as the sky above.*

Bateman's Bay, New South Wales. Situated on the south-east coast, the bay tends to be home to flocks of pelicans. Here, on a cold winter's morning, they appear to be totally at home, bathing and preening while a fishing vessel returns to port.

The Great Ocean Road follows the coastline for much of its 200 kilometre length from Torquay to Peterborough. In some places it is the only thing separating the mountains and the rock formations on the coast. Facing the southern ocean, majestic, weatherworn landforms provide

a spectacular view. Here, the resilient Twelve Apostles - sentinels that have stood above the cold ocean for countless years - shrink beneath sunset shadows.

Jutting rock formations that confront the surging power of the ocean are typical along the Victorian coast. During the ongoing conflict between land and sea, unpredictable white swells often shatter themselves upon these slippery rocks.

Sometimes the danger of the ocean's pulling force is not a sufficient deterrent for coastal enthusiasts. Many people risk their lives fishing from such places.

Today, Port Arthur is a beautiful picnic spot, with vast lawns and sandstone ruins, "a Roman Forum sprawling over 40 hectares on the Tasman Sea". But from 1830 to 1877, it was a prison for about 12,500 convicts from across the British Empire.

From within Freycinet National Park, this view across Coles Bay looks towards the main part of the island near Swansea on the east coast of Tasmania. Illuminated by midday light, the rich colours of the outcrop reach towards the faint coastline in the distance. Thick, sugar-white clouds fill a slice of Australian sky.

On account of its captivating beauty, Freycinet National Park in Tasmania has been the subject of many poems, particularly by James McAuley. Here, its pink granite cliffs and dazzling blue sea are captured in the muted tones of an early morning winter chill.

Wineglass Bay, within the Freycinet National Park, is a photographer's delight because of the almost-perfect crescent shape of its white sand beach. High, imposing headlands form its outer edges, and the bay is backed by an unspoilt wilderness of trees, shrubs and wildflowers.

Point Leveque, Broome, Kimberley Region, Western Australia
As this landform greets the Indian Ocean, the ore-inlayed soil of Australia's north

west is shown to be a rich, red ochre colour. Wild tides, reaching ten metres in
some instances, make navigation hazardous along this part of the coast.

Mindil Beach, Darwin, Northern Territory. Australia's northern-most city, Darwin is a developing metropolis with a distinct cosmopolitan flavour. Ingredients that give Darwin flair and an easy-going lifestyle include its cultural mix, savage climate, tropical coastline, and its experience of man-made and natural disasters. Mindil, shown here at sunset, is famous for its Darwin Beer Can Regatta, held each August.

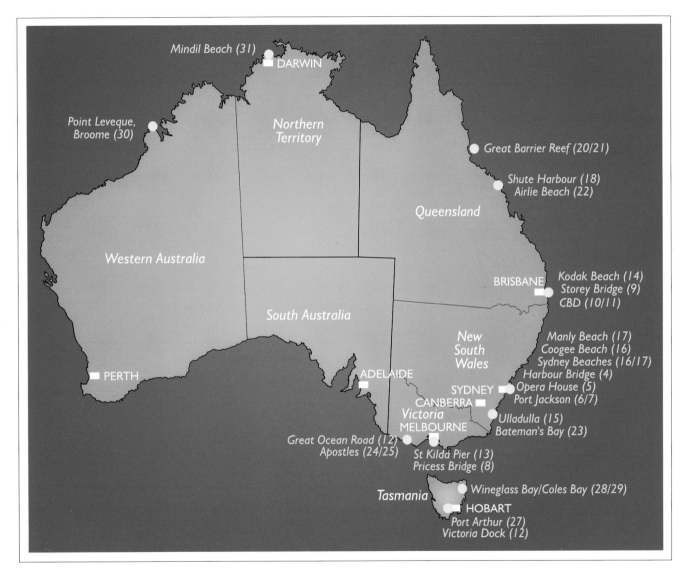

Mindil Beach (31)
DARWIN

Point Leveque,
Broome (30)

Northern
Territory

Great Barrier Reef (20/21)

Shute Harbour (18)
Airlie Beach (22)

Queensland

Western Australia

South Australia

Kodak Beach (14)
Storey Bridge (9)
CBD (10/11)
BRISBANE

New
South
Wales

Manly Beach (17)
Coogee Beach (16)
Sydney Beaches (16/17)
Harbour Bridge (4)
Opera House (5)
Port Jackson (6/7)

ADELAIDE

PERTH

SYDNEY
CANBERRA

Victoria
MELBOURNE

Ulladulla (15)
Bateman's Bay (23)

Great Ocean Road (12)
Apostles (24/25)

St Kilda Pier (13)
Pricess Bridge (8)

Tasmania

Wineglass Bay/Coles Bay (28/29)

HOBART

Port Arthur (27)
Victoria Dock (12)

Little Hills Press Pty Ltd
Sydney, Australia
ACN 002 648 393
ISBN 1863151397
email: info@littlehills.com
http:\\www.littlehills.com

Concept: Chris Baker
Design and Development - Artitude
Initial picture selection: Vincent Wijangco
Editorial Team: Sam Lynch, Mark Truman
Front Cover: Shute Harbour,
Great Barrier Reef, Queensland
Back Cover: Detail of 12 Apostles, Victoria

Photograph Credits:
Australian Tourist Commission -
        pages 2-3, 13, 30.
Eduard Domin pages 4, 5, 15, 16, 18, 19, 20-21
        22, 23, 24, 25, 26, 27, 28, 29.
Chris Baker 8, 12.
Queensland Tourist Authority 9, 10-11, 14.
Tourism NSW 17.
Northern Territory Tourist Commission 31.
Darren Houpton 6, 7.

Printed in Korea